WEAPONS & EQUIPMENT OF THE GERMAN CAVALRY

1935-1945

KLAUS RICHTER

Schiffer Military History
Atglen, PA

German cavalry troop during the war in Russia. The troopers wear the garrison cap for NCOs and men, second form with soutache, and carry the Kar 98k carbine slung across their backs. The new-style saddlebags are attached behind the saddle. The horses carry forage bags on their chests.

BIBLIOGRAPHY

H.Dv. 299/2, 3, 6a and 10, 1937-39.

OKH-Waffenhefte des Heeres, Schnelle Truppen Teil II o.J.

Springer, Major, Dr.: Reiterkrieg (Cavalry War), 1944.

Der General der Infanterie im OKH - I Kav.: Überblick über die Entwicklung der deutschen Kavallerie vor und in diesem Kriege (Survey of the Development of the German Cavalry before and during This War), February 1945.

von Stein, H.R., Major (Rtd.): Die deutsche Kavallerie 1939-1945), in Feldgrau 1955.

Oberst (Rtd) von Rauchhaupt, Wilhelm Volrad: Die Deutsche Kavallerie zwischen den beiden letzten Kriegen (The German Cavalry between the Last Two Wars), 1958.

von Senger und Etterlin Jr., Dr. F.M.: Die 24. Panzer Division vormals 1. Kavallerie-Division (The 24th Panzer Division, Formerly the 1st Cavalry Division), 1962.

Tessin, Georg: Verbände and Truppen der deutschen Wehrmacht und Waffen-SS 1939-1945 (Units and Troops of the German Armed Forces and Waffen-SS 1939-1945), 1962.

Richter, Klaus Christian: Die Geschichte der deutschen Kavallerie 1919-1945 (The History of the German Cavalry 1919-1945), 1978 and 1982.

The majority of the photographs and drawings in this book are from the author's collection.

Additional photos were provided by
Rittmeister (Rtd.) Conrad Müller, formerly of the 2nd (Prussian) Horse Regiment and Cavalry Regiment Center, and
Rittmeister (Rtd.) Heiner Schubert, formerly of the 6th Cavalry Regiment and the 34th Reconnaissance Battalion.

Translated from the German by David Johnston.

Copyright © 1995 by Schiffer Publishing Ltd.

All rights reserved. No part of this work may be reproduced or used in any forms or by any means – graphic, electronic or mechanical, including photocopying or information storage and retrieval systems – without written permission from the copyright holder.

Printed in the United States of America.
ISBN: 0-88740-816-8

This book was originally published under the title,
Waffen und Ausrüstung der Deutschen Kavallerie 1935-1945,
by Podzun-Pallas Verlag.

We are interested in hearing from authors with book ideas on related topics.

Published by Schiffer Publishing Ltd.
77 Lower Valley Road
Atglen, PA 19310
Please write for a free catalog.
This book may be purchased from the publisher.
Please include $2.95 postage.
Try your bookstore first.

INTRODUCTION

With passage of the law for the building-up of the Armed Forces (Wehrmacht) on March 16, 1945, the Reichswehr, the so-called 100,000-man army, became the foundation stone for the future Wehrmacht. The Reichswehr was a volunteer army, and every detail of its composition, along with numerous limitations and bans, had been imposed on the former German Reich by the Treaty of Versailles. The Reichswehr was allocated a numerically-large cavalry, with a ratio of twenty-one infantry to eighteen cavalry regiments. In terms of personnel the cavalry made up 16.4% of the entire army, while the artillery's share was fixed at only 10.9%. This relatively large cavalry force was taken into the new Wehrmacht along with the other seven branches of the service.

The first, though partly still camouflaged, restructuring of the army took place in 1934. The object of the changes was the creation of a large, modern army. Two horse regiments had to give up their mounts as part of these measures. The units were motorized and formed the cadres for the 1st and 3rd Rifle Regiments as well as the 1st, 2nd and 3rd Motorcycle Battalions. In the course of the year 1935 the 2nd, 3rd and 6th Panzer Regiments were formed from three further horse regiments and various individual cavalry units.

The Wehrmacht was thus initially left with thirteen horse regiments. They were quickly brought back up to their original strengths as a result of the introduction of universal compulsory military service on May 21, 1935 and the incorporation of mounted formations of the State Police.

Two horse regiments which had been motorized or reorganized as panzer units in 1934-35 were reformed as cavalry regiments in 1936 and 1938 respectively.

When World War Two broke out in 1939 the Wehrmacht had at its disposal fifteen predominantly horse-mounted cavalry regiments. Also part of the cavalry arm in 1939 were the 1st Bicycle Battalion, the armored reconnaissance battalions and regiments, and the cavalry-riflemen. As the armored reconnaissance units became a component of the armored command, and the cavalry-riflemen (later just riflemen, and renamed panzer-grenadiers in 1942) joined the infantry, they are not included in the following account.

The cavalry of the Reichswehr was armed with the 3.2-meter steel-tube lance with lance pennant until October 3, 1927. After the lance was "put on the shelf" the cavalry was developed into a mobile firearm-equipped force.

THE DEVELOPMENT OF THE CAVALRY WITHIN THE REBUILDING OF THE ARMY 1935-1939

The eighteen horse regiments of the Reichswehr were organized into three cavalry divisions, whose heavy weapons consisted essentially of one heavy machine-gun platoon per regiment and a battalion of horse artillery per division. The terms of the Treaty of Versailles did not permit the required strengthening and modernization of these divisions; therefore, Germany freed herself from the conditions of the treaty step by step.

The reattainment of unrestricted military sovereignty in 1935 paved the way for a modernized, heavily-armed and suitably organized cavalry.

Since the roles of the former Army Cavalry had largely been taken over by the mechanized forces, the Wehrmacht retained only a single army cavalry unit, the 1st (East-Prussian) Cavalry Brigade, whose role was that of a experimental unit. It used the horse for rapid, long-ranging movements over any terrain for as long as possible before dismounting and then conducting the fight on foot like the infantry.

The bulk of the cavalry, however, was organized into regiments which incorporated horse-mounted, bicycle-mounted and motorized units. Each of these units was placed under the direct command of one of the army's non-motorized army corps.

In contrast to the two horse regiments of the 1st Cavalry Brigade, during peacetime the cavalry regiments were responsible for forming reconnaissance battalions for secondment to infantry and alpine divisions in the event of mobilization.

Given the marching speed of the infantry, tactical reconnaissance, one of the essential missions of the cavalry, could still be carried out successfully by men on horseback or bicycles. Those cavalry formations and units tasked with this mission were designated as Troop Cavalry.

During the period 1936-1939 the units of the army cavalry and the troop cavalry were to a large extent armed and equipped like the infantry, as the production capacity of the armaments industry allowed. The only differences were those dictated by the nature of the horse and the bicycle. On foot the trooper was now supposed to be indistinguishable from the infantryman; consequently, both used the same combat training manual. The rapid change from riding to shooting was seen as the essence of cavalry warfare.

The cavalry rode, in order to be able to shoot from the proper area of the battlefield at the right time, and it used its arms so that it could ride again, which meant freeing itself for further employment in a mobile role.

Field parade by the 1st (Horse) Battalion, 13th Cavalry Regiment in front of the regimental commander. The saddles are held in place by web girths and martingales. The latter were done away with in 1941.

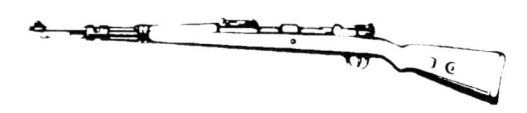

Left: The Wehrmacht cavalryman differed considerably from the infantryman in outward appearance with his breeches, riding boots with spurs and trooper's pack from the Type 34 saddlebag.

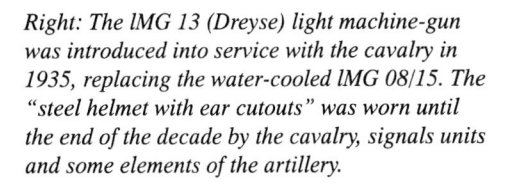

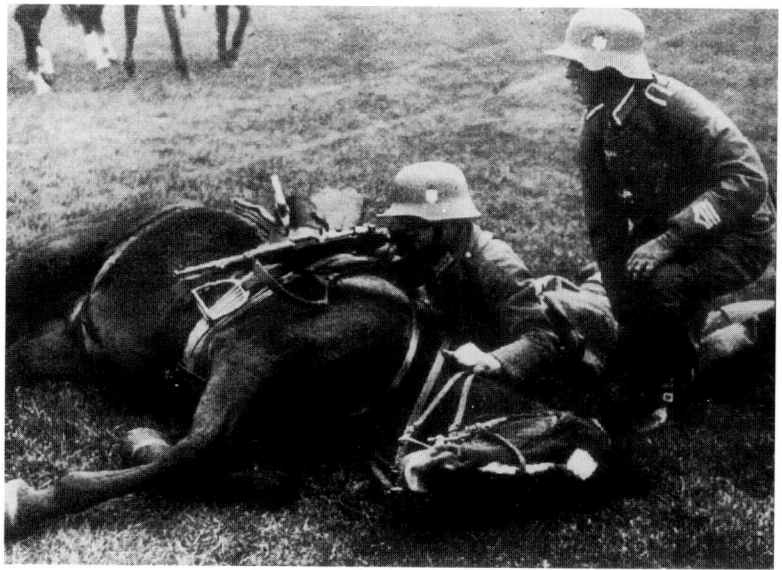

Right: The lMG 13 (Dreyse) light machine-gun was introduced into service with the cavalry in 1935, replacing the water-cooled lMG 08/15. The "steel helmet with ear cutouts" was worn until the end of the decade by the cavalry, signals units and some elements of the artillery.

*Left and above right:
The Karabiner 98k carbine was originally developed solely for horse-mounted and horse-drawn troops. It became the standard weapon of the German Armed Forces on account of its ease of use and outstanding ballistic characteristics. Seen here: M 18 steel helmet and cavalry helmet side by side in the same troop.*

Above and right:
The water-cooled sMG 08 continued in use as a heavy machine-gun. It was loaded on a machine-gun wagon with front limber and was transported by a team of six horses.

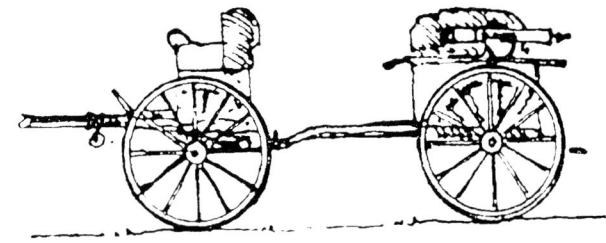

Left:
The lMG 13 (Dreyse) and the sMG 08 were both replaced by the MG 34 in 1936. The new weapon could be used as a light machine-gun with bipod and as a heavy machine-gun with gun mount. (15th Cavalry Regiment)

Above and below left:
The machine-gun half-squad carried the light version of the MG 34 and its ammunition boxes on the saddle. The photo offers of a good view of the enlisted man's saber and the ammunition boxes in the right-side saddlebags. (13th Cavalry Regiment)

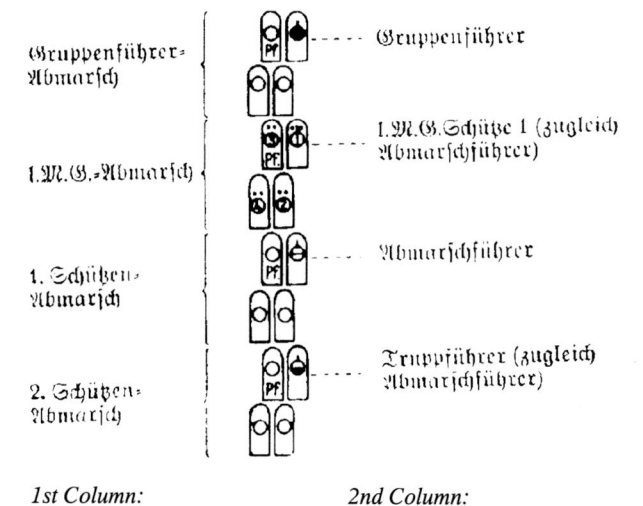

1st Column:
Squad leader - half-squad
light machine-gun half-squad
1st gunner - half-squad
2nd gunner - half-squad

2nd Column:
Squad leader
Light machine-gun 1st gunner (also half-squad leader)
Half-squad leader
Section leader (also half-squad leader)

Right:
Removing the lMG 34 from its scabbard mounted on the left side of the saddle behind the rider.

7

Above:
The heavy machine gun with gun mount and its ammunition boxes were carried in two loads on the Type 33 pack saddle. (13th Cavalry Regiment)

Left:
The MG 34, here the light version with drum feed, continued in use until the end of the war, even after the introduction of the MG 42.

The machine-gun section of a horse troop unloading its equipment.

Above and right:
Troop commander, squadron headquarters squad leader, three platoon commanders, nine squad leaders and the machine-gun section leader were equipped with the MPi 38. (6th Cavalry Regiment)

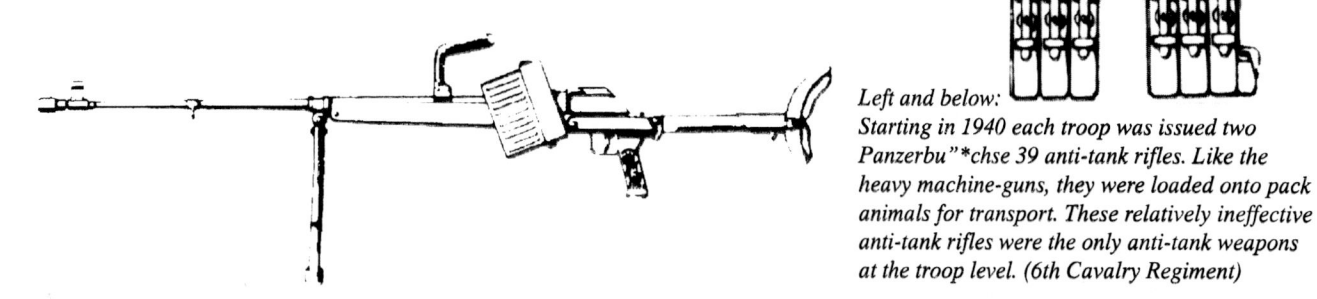

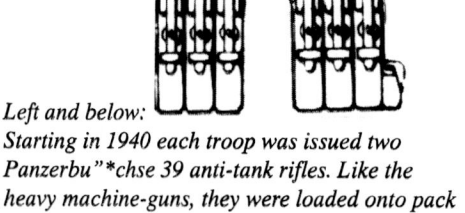

Left and below:
*Starting in 1940 each troop was issued two Panzerbu"*chse 39 anti-tank rifles. Like the heavy machine-guns, they were loaded onto pack animals for transport. These relatively ineffective anti-tank rifles were the only anti-tank weapons at the troop level. (6th Cavalry Regiment)*

9

The MPi 38 was later replaced by the MPi 40, which used stamped metal parts in its manufacture. The reconnaissance battalions raised during the war also used other types of submachine-gun. The Wachtmeister in this photo carries a Steyr Soloturn S1-100. Note the cord girth, already phased out by the active peacetime units.

The carbine, the standard weapon of the trooper, was carried in the carbine scabbard carrier on the left side of the saddle behind the rider. These cavalrymen are still equipped with Type 26 saddlebags, which were later replaced by the Type 34. (3rd Cavalry Regiment)

Below: From 1941 the carbine was carried slung across the trooper's back. The NCO is armed with a MPi 40. As the photo clearly shows, during the war there was no standard method of packing the gear stowed behind the saddle. (15th Cavalry Regiment)

Right:
There were two versions of the carbine scabbard carrier. Here the older version, in which a strap held the butt of the rifle in the carrier pocket.

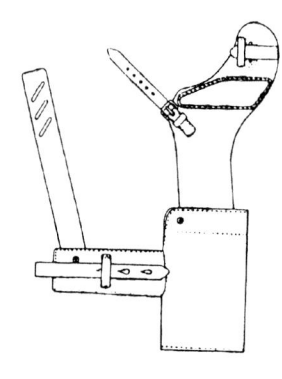

Above:
This is how the carbine was carried while "dismounting for combat." The carbine retaining strap attached the weapon to the rider's belt while he was in the saddle. (13th Cavalry Regiment)

Below:
Carbine retaining strap.

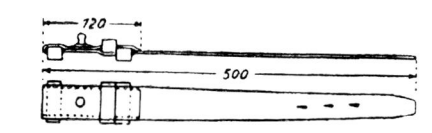

Left:
Carbine scabbard carrier.

Right:
Dismounted cavalry with "carbines at heel." (15th Cavalry Regiment).

Left:
The Type 25 army saddle with Type 34 saddlebags and rear saddle pack.

Right:
Packed according to the manual: the rear saddle pack, consisting of the rider's forage bag and rolled-up greatcoat or tent square. (6th Cavalry Regiment)

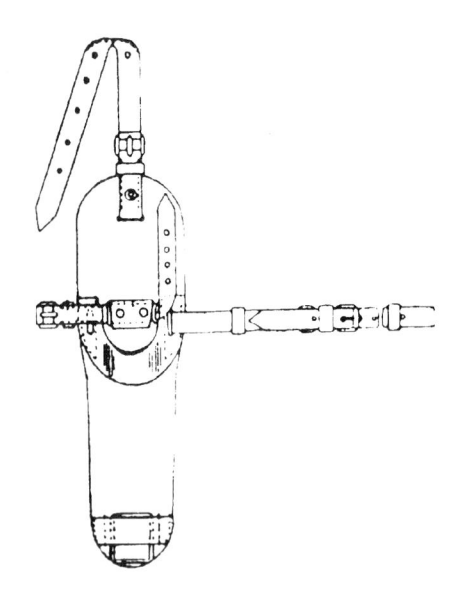

Above:
The saber scabbard.

Left:
Riding breeches with leather trim. The Type 25 army saddle is still equipped with the cord girth. In addition to shoulder straps, the Oberwachtmeister on the horse is wearing the rank badges for fatigue jacket on his sleeve.

Below: The enlisted man's saber in saber scabbard on the right side of the saddle behind the rider. The trooper in the foreground has his folding spade in a carrying pouch with closing clasp cover.

Right:
This photo illustrates how troopers carried their equipment while on the march. (15th Cavalry Regiment)

Left and below:
The horse was not considered a weapon by the Wehrmacht. To every horse-mounted or horse-drawn unit, however, its mobility in almost any terrain and season made it more than just a means of transportation. The provinces of East Prussia and Hanover provided most of the saddle horses. Later, during the war, horses from many European countries were used.

The horse in the above photograph is an East-Prussian Trakehner, that in the photo on the right is a Hanoveraner.
The Wehrmacht used as a saddle underpad a coarse folded wool blanket, whose official designation was Woilach (see above photo). The Gefreiter (lance corporal) on the right is using a privately-purchased saddle blanket.

*Left:
Beginning in 1936, a growing number of bicycle and motor troops joined the cavalry.*

*Right:
In each cavalry regiment the Ist (Horse) Battalion was joined by a IInd (Bicycle) Battalion, which was partially motorized. (18th Cavalry Regiment)*

*Left:
The standard service bicycle as per H.Dv. 293 of December 13, 1935.*

A bicycle troop on the move displays the typical carriage of equipment. The two lowest ranks in these units were Reiter and Oberreiter, the same as the horse-mounted units.

Below: Each bicycle troop included a motorcycle section, which transported the heavy machine-guns and 50-mm light mortars. (13th Cavalry Regiment)

Live firing practice with the 50-mm mortar. It was anticipated that in combat each bicycle platoon would be supported by high-angle fire provided by a light mortar. (6th Cavalry Regiment)

The heaviest weapon possessed by the horse and cavalry regiments was the Light Infantry Gun 18 (lIG 18), which was designated as "cavalry gun" by the troopers. Horse regiments had four of these weapons in their 5th (Heavy) Troops and cavalry regiments six in their 10th (Heavy) Troops. The lIG 18 had a caliber of 75 mm and was capable of extremely accurate high-angle and flat-trajectory fire. The cavalry gun was therefore also used in an anti-tank role, especially by the reconnaissance battalions.

An anti-tank platoon with three 37-mm anti-tank guns was integrated into the Headquarters Troop of each horse regiment; in contrast, cavalry regiments had a 9th (Anti-tank) Troop with six guns.

The cavalry regiments used the Kfz 69, the so-called "Krupp-Protze," to transport their cavalry and anti-tank guns. This vehicle, which was produced until 1942, was very popular with the troops.

In the horse regiments the cavalry gun was pulled by a team of six horses. Accordingly it and its associated front limber were fitted with spoked wheels.

Below: A cavalry gun in firing position.

The first armored cars joined the cavalry in 1934, a sign of what was to come. The headquarters troop of each horse regiment included an armored reconnaissance section; each cavalry regiment possessed an armored reconnaissance platoon consisting of three armored reconnaissance sections as part of its 10th (Heavy) Troop. An armored reconnaissance section consisted of two machine-gun-armed Kfz 13 armored cars and a Kfz 14 radio car. (13th Cavalry Regiment)

Left and below: Kfz 13 armored cars wearing solid white Balkenkreuze during the war in Poland, and...

..with the style of cross introduced in 1940.

21

Bugler corps and 1st Troop of the 14th Cavalry Regiment in Berlin on June 2, 1939 on the occasion of the last parade held before the Second World War. The buglers also carry a signalling bugle on their backs.
Below:
Kettledrummer with drum draperies. Tack and saddle blanket as laid down in the regulations of 2/11/1937. Only drum horses were adorned in this way. (6th Cavalry Regiment)

Below:
Buglers were employed as an acoustical signalling resource during maneuvers and in the war. (1st Horse Regiment)

Kettledrummer and bugler corps of the 14th Cavalry Regiment, backed up by buglers of the 12th Artillery Regiment. Drum draperies and fanfare flags according to the regulations in place in the period 1929-1933, which allowed plenty of leeway in their design.

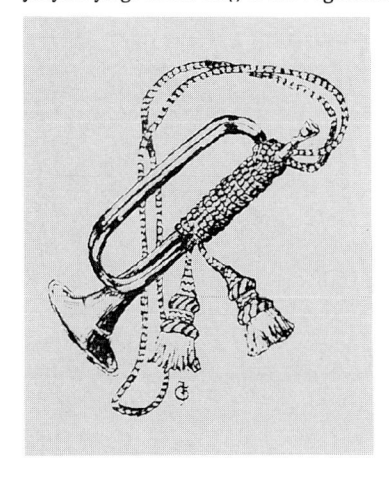

The signalling bugle.

*Right:
The bugler corps was not just a parade unit, rather it was a full participant in all exercises and maneuvers.*

Above:
All horse and cavalry regiments were awarded standards during the period 1936-38.

Above left: The standard bearer was distinguished by the "Badge for Flag and Standard Bearer." It was worn on the upper part of the right sleeve. (18th Cavalry Regiment)

Below:
The standard party on horseback. (15th Cavalry Regiment)

Below:
While on duty with the standard, the standard bearer wore a gorget and bandolier. (6th Cavalry Regiment)

24

Above:
The saber was the identifying and distinguishing weapon of all horse-mounted troops until 1941. Seen here is the officer's saber. Also visible is the right third of the martingale and the S-shaped curb-bit. (18th Cavalry Regiment)

Right:
Cavalryman in the tunic with "Brandenburg" cuffs and private saber. Introduced in 1936, this pocketless extra coat was referred to irreverently as the "Hindenburg Tunic," "Kaiser Wilhelm Memorial Tunic," or simply "Sarrasani," after a very well-known circus of the day. (15th Cavalry Regiment)

Parades were ridden with "sabers up!" (3rd Cavalry Regiment)

Right:
The enlisted man's saber was similar in shape and weight to the former artillery saber of the old army. One of the measures to be taken on mobilization was sharpening the edge.

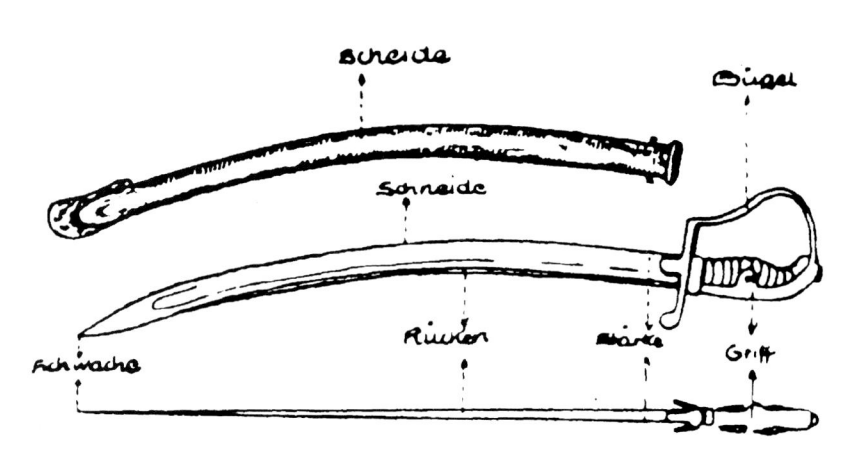

Left:
As before, in combat the saber served as a weapon of attack.

Right:
A horse regiment's combat train consisted of an Hf 1 ammunition and weapons wagon, a large blacksmith wagon and a field kitchen. Other horse-drawn vehicles and individual motor vehicles joined the train in wartime. This Hf 1 wears Reichswehr camouflage colors.

Type 25 harness with Type 25 army saddle (for armed forces team of horses)

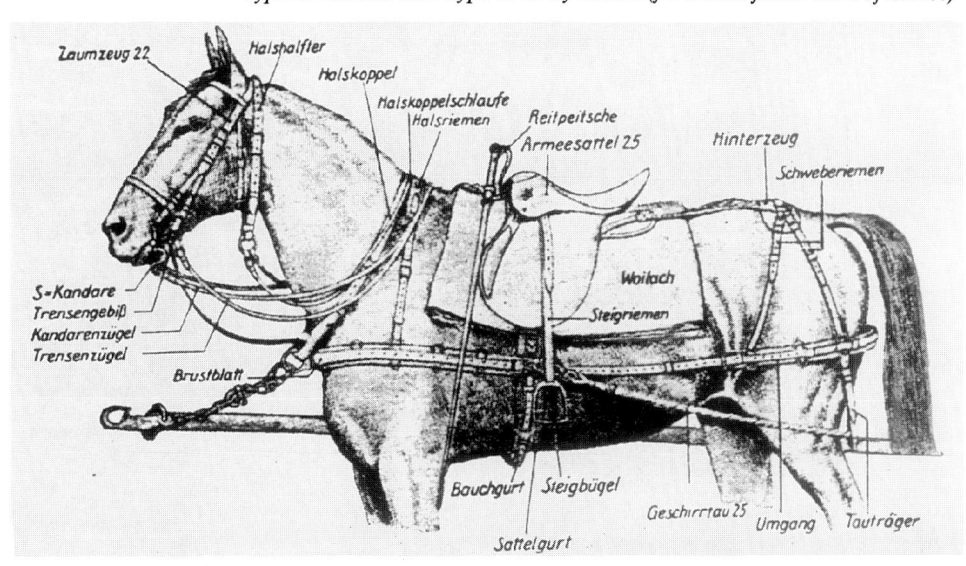

Below:
The blacksmith wagon unloaded.

27

Left:
The field kitchen was driven behind a front limber. During the war a six-horse team frequently had to be used. (5th Cavalry Regiment)

Right:
The great advantage of this field kitchen, in addition to its ease of operation, was the ability to cook food while on the move.

Left:
In the field horses were fed from a so-called forage-bag, which was in fact a watering bag made of waterproof duck. (6th Cavalry Regiment)

28

Above: In 1938 the six Austrian Dragoon Troops were incorporated into the German Armed Forces. Their uniform was distinguished by a "fur piece" which was wore over the left shoulder. These troops formed the 11th Cavalry regiment based at Stockerau near Vienna.

Right: Horse inspection. The photo shows the various types of uniform worn by the cavalry in the course of its daily service routine.

Left: River crossing with pneumatic floats as laid down in H.Dv. 316 (All.Pi.D.). The manual did not use the term "inflatable boat." The troopers are wearing the garrison cap for NCOs and men, first form, from 1934 without the national eagle.

The 15 Cavalry Regiments of the Wehrmacht
As of 1939 (before the outbreak of war) - Designations - Bases - Commanders - Maintenance of Traditions

1st Horse Regiment
Base: Insterburg (East Prussia)
Commander: Oberst Frhr. v. Esebeck.
Maintenance of Traditions: Rgt. HQ, HQ troop and 1st Troop: 1st Dragoon Rgt.; 2nd and 5th Troops: 8th Uhlan Rgt.; 3rd Troop: 12th Uhlan Rgt.; 4th Heavy Troop: 9th Light Horse Infantry Rgt.

2nd Horse Regiment
Base: Angerburg (East Prussia)
Commander: Oberstlt. v. Saucken.
Maintenance of Traditions: Rgt. HQ, HQ Troop and 5th Troop: 4th Uhlan Rgt.; 1st and 4th Troops: 5th Cuirassier Rgt.; 2nd and 3rd Troops: 10th Light Horse Infantry Rgt.

3rd Cavalry Regiment
Base: Göttingen (in the RW: Rathenow and Stendal)
Commander: Oberstlt. v. Senger und Etterlin.
Maintenance of Traditions: Rgt. HQ and 2nd Troop: 3rd Hussar Rgt.; 1st Troop: 6th Cuirassier Rgt.; 3rd Troop: 14th Hussar Rgt.; 4th Troop: 6th Dragoons Rgt.; 5th Heavy Troop: 7th Uhlan Rgt.

4th Cavalry Regiment
Base: Allenstein (East Prussia) 4th and 7th Troops temporarily Osterode (East Prussia), 8th Troop temporarily Stablack Troop Training Grounds.
Commander: Oberstlt. v. Heydebrand und der Lasa.
Maintenance of Traditions: Ist Btl.: 10th and 11th Dragoons Rgts.

5th Cavalry Regiment
Base: Stolp (Pomerania)
Commander in Chief: Generalfeldmarschall von Mackensen.
Commanding Officer: Oberstlt. Diener.
Maintenance of Traditions: Rgt. HQ, 1st, 5th and 11th Troops: 1st Bodyguard Hussars Rgt.; HQ Ist Btl., 2nd Troop and 4th Heavy Troop: 2nd Bodyguard Hussars Rgt.; 3rd Troop and IInd Battalion: 5th Hussars Rgt.

6th Cavalry Regiment
Base: Darmstadt, HQ IInd Btl., 7th, 8th and 10th Troops temporarily Bensheim (Bergstrasse), later also Darmstadt (in the RW: Pasewalk, Schwedt/Oder, Demmin)
Commanding Officer: Oberst v. Lenski.
Maintenance of Traditions: Rgt. HQ, 1st and 7th Troops: 23rd (Hesse) Guards Dragoons Rgt.; HQ Ist Btl., 4th, 5th and 8th Troops: 24th (Hesse) Bodyguard Dragoon Rgt.; 2nd, 9th and 10th Troops: 7th Dragoons Rgt.; HQ IInd Btl., 3rd and 6th Troops: 13th Hussars Regiment.

8th Cavalry Regiment
Base: Oels (Silesia), 4th Troop Namslau.
Commanding Officer: Oberstlt. v. Einsiedel.
Maintenance of Traditions: Rgt. HQ, Ist Btl. and 11th Troop: 8th Dragoons Rgt.; IInd Btl.: 1st Uhlan Rgt.

9th Cavalry Regiment
Base: Fürstenwalde (Spree)
Commanding Officer: Oberstlt. Hartenbeck.
Maintenance of Traditions: Rgt. HQ, Ist Btl. and 11th Troop: 3rd Uhlan Rgt.; 1st Troop: 1st Guards Dragoons Rgt.; 5th troop: 2nd Guards Dragoons Rgt.; IInd Btl.: 3rd Horse Grenadier Rgt. (3rd Dragoons Rgt.).

10th Cavalry Regiment
Base: Torgau (Elbe).
Commanding Officer: Oberst Krüger.
Maintenance of Traditions: Rgt. HQ, Ist Btl. and 11th Troop: 12th Hussars Rgt., IInd Btl.: 7th Cuirassier Rgt.

11th Cavalry Regiment
Base: Stockerau (near Vienna).
Commanding Officer: Oberstlt. v. Hülsen.
Maintenance of Traditions: the purely German regiments of the k.u.k. Austro-Hungarian Cavalry, the maintenance of whose traditions following the collapse of 1918 was assumed by the six Dragoon Troops of the new Federal Army of the Republic of Austria (German Austria) until the beginning of 1938, specifically: 3rd Lower-Austrian Dragoons Rgt., 4th Upper-Austrian Salzburg Dragoons Rgt., 5th Steyr-Carinthia-Krainer Dragoons Rgt., 11th Moravian Dragoons Rgt., 15th Lower-Austrian-Moravian Dragoons Rgt., and the Mounted Tirolean Regional Defense Division (honorarily renamed the "The Mounted Tirolean Emperor's Riflemen" in 1917).

13th Cavalry Regiment
Base: Lüneburg.
Commanding Officer: Oberstlt. v. Randow.
Maintenance of Traditions: Ist Btl.: 9th and 16th Dragoons Rgts., 13th and 16th Uhlan Regiments; IInd Btl.: 17th Hussars Rgt.

14th Cavalry Regiment
Base: Ludwigslust, Ist Btl. Parchim.
Commanding Officer: Oberstlt. v. Arnim.
Maintenance of Traditions: Rgt. HQ, IInd Btl. and 11th Troop: 17th Dragoons Rgt., Ist Btl.: 18th Dragoons Rgt., 3rd Troop: 16th Hussars Rgt., 4th Troop: 13th Dragoons Rgt.

15th Cavalry Regiment
Base: Paderborn (Westphalia), Ist Btl. Neuhaus (Paderborn District)
Commanding Officer: Oberst Baron Digeon v. Monteton.
Maintenance of Traditions: Rgt. HQ, 5th, 9th and 11th Troops: 8th Hussars Rgt., 1st and 6th Troops: 7th Hussars Rgt., 2nd and 7th Troops: 4th Cuirassier Rgt., 3rd, 8th and 10th Troops: 11th Hussars Rgt.

17th Cavalry Regiment
Base: Bamberg.
Commanding Officer: Oberst Fremerey.
Maintenance of Traditions: KB 2 2nd Troop Horse Regiment, KB 1 Uhlan Rgt., 4th and 8th Troops Chev. Rgt.

18th Cavalry Regiment
Base: Stuttgart-Bad Cannstadt, HQ IInd Btl., 9th, 10th and 11th Troops Bruchsal (Baden). The regiment is to be unified in Bruchsal in 1940.
Commanding Officer: Oberst Voigt.
Maintenance of Traditions: Ist Btl.: 25th and 26th Dragoons Rgts., 19th and 20th Uhlan Rgts.; IInd Btl.: 20th Dragoon Rgt.

THE CAVALRY AT WAR

In the course of mobilization in 1939 the eighteen cavalry regiments formed thirty-eight reconnaissance battalions for the first wave of divisions and sixteen for the second wave. As well, in individual cases there were detachments in the form of infantry horse platoons to infantry regiments which did not have these partial units in peacetime and cadres for the reconnaissance battalions of the fourth wave.

Each cavalry regiment left behind a reconnaissance training and replacement battalion at its peacetime base and these units carried on the number of the former cavalry regiment. Thus it cannot be said that the cavalry regiments were completely disbanded at the start of the war. The mission of the reconnaissance training and replacement battalions was to provide the units formed from their former regiments with trained replacement personnel and horses as required and to establish additional reconnaissance formations and units.

The reconnaissance battalions proved themselves very well while operating within their divisions during the first campaigns of the Second World War, though understandably a unit which employed three different modes of transport ¨- horse, bicycle, motor vehicle ¨-was not easy to command.

Organized into patrols, the battalion reconnoitered ahead of its division's front and flanks, with the horse-mounted patrols for the most part operating off firm roads, while the bicycle patrols were usually tied to these. The reconnaissance battalion's armored car patrol, which consisted of three vehicles, represented an infantry division's only armored vehicles in the early years of the war. To it were assigned the more distant reconnaissance objectives.

If force of arms was required to carry out a reconnaissance mission, the troops were committed as a body with the support of the heavy weapons. The battalions' motorized and bicycle units were also frequently used to form the basis of various types of advance detachment. When this took place the division's only remaining reconnaissance asset was the horse troop.

The onset of the muddy period in Russia in the autumn of 1941 demonstrated the unsuitability of combining horse-mounted and bicycle troops. While the bicycle became a burden, and those that were left could no longer be used, it was the horse which enabled the reconnaissance battalion to retain its mobility. After the German advance came to a halt, which reduced reconnaissance to a relatively minor role, the reconnaissance battalions inevitably became mobile reserves for their divisions. They subsequently earned the honorary title "division fire-brigade." In the course of 1942 the reconnaissance battalions were largely decimated in their role as helpers in emergency situations.

The 1st (East-Prussian) Cavalry Brigade proved that army cavalry still had a role to play while operating as an experimental unit in the campaign against Poland. The brigade was transferred to the Königsbrück troop Training Grounds in Saxony immediately after this "campaign of the eighteen days" and there was expanded into the 1st Cavalry Division. As such it saw action in Holland, Belgium and France. For Operation Barbarossa in June 1942 it was placed under the command of Panzergruppe 2 commanded by General Guderian. The cavalry division proved fully able to match the offensive tempo of the panzer divisions, though it required a maximum effort. In late autumn 1941 the sole army cavalry unit was reequipped and became the 24th Panzer Division.

The 1-3 horse-mounted patrol was one of the most important missions of the cavalry.

The three armored cars of the reconnaissance battalion —for the most part still the Kfz 13, dubbed the bathtub on account of its shape —were the sole armored vehicles of the infantry divisions at the start of the war. (15th Cavalry Regiment)

Crossing the River Bug by pneumatic float. This procedure was not a simple one, even for the active cavalry units. The trooper wears a fitting on his Stahlhelm 35 helmet for the attachment of camouflage material, a sort of predecessor to the camouflage net.

Cooperation between horse-mounted and armored car patrols. On the right rear fender of the armored car is the tactical symbol for the troop of a reconnaissance battalion, on the left the battalion unit emblem.

Below: The last reconnaissance battalions to be formed often had a motorcycle instead of an armored car section; it saw less but could be heard at a distance.

Left:
A bicycle troop of the 1st Bicycle Battalion during the campaign in Western Europe in 1940. Carbines were no longer worn slung across the back, instead they were carried on the crossbar of the bicycle. (1st Cavalry Division)

Right:
Those reconnaissance battalions which had neither armored cars nor motorcycles had to carry out their duties using standard civilian automobiles. (6th Cavalry Regiment)

Left: The horse-mounted patrols proved especially valuable in the difficult terrain conditions that prevailed in the east. Seen here is an improvised horse-mounted patrol of the 36th Motorized Reconnaissance Battalion, photographed on 22/8/1941 during the advance on Leningrad. The riders wear no specialized riding equipment and they are mounted on captured Russian horses. (6th Cavalry Regiment)

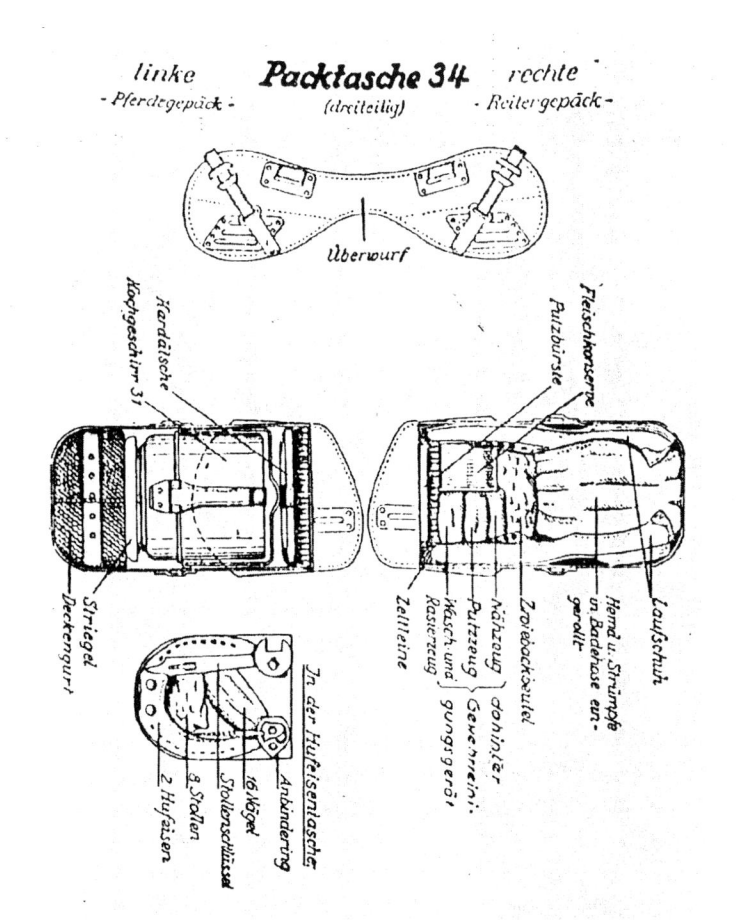

Above: Packtasche 34 saddlebags. As well as the German Army's standard S-bit, curb bits with straight bars were often used, especially by new formations.

Trooper with the standard equipment of 1941. The carbine scabbard carrier has disappeared, while the "new style" saddlebags are worn behind the saddle. (1st Cavalry Division)

*Below:
The new saddlebag introduced on 15/2/1940.*

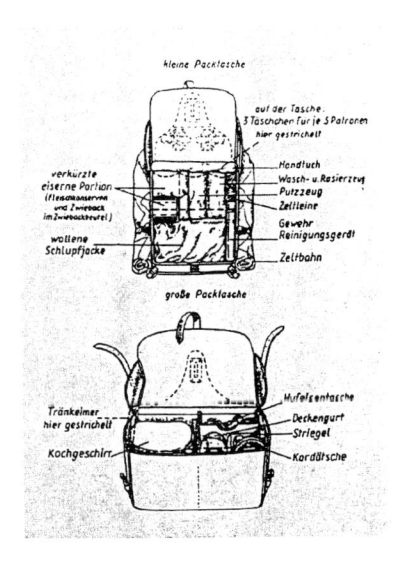

35

Above:
Carriage of saddlebags and rear pack during the French Campaign in 1940. The horse had a considerable amount of "dead weight" to carry in addition to the rider. (6th Cavalry Regiment)

Left:
The ammunition section of a horse troop's machine-gun platoon in Russia 1941. (8th Cavalry Regiment)

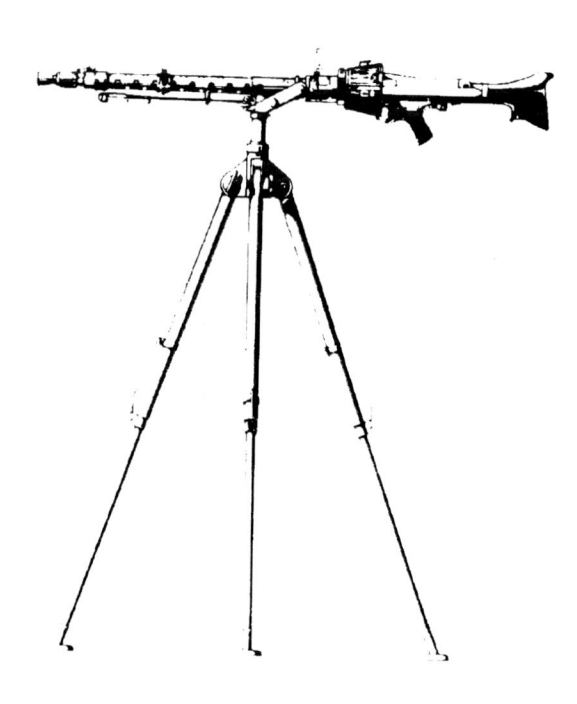

In the beginning each MG 34 came with a tripod for use in the anti-aircraft role; however, as of 1941 each horse platoon carried with it only a single tripod. (6th Cavalry Regiment)

Below: The commander of the 2nd (Bicycle) Troop in his B-Krad (motorcycle with sidecar). On the front of the sidecar is the tactical symbol for a troop of this type. Russia 1941. (6th Cavalry Regiment)

37

Left:
Squad leader and machine-gun half-squad with typical arms and equipment. Russia 1942. (6th Cavalry Regiment)

Right:
A horse troop at rest with unloaded machine-gun. Even though pack horses had been introduced in 1939 to transport the MG 34 and its ammunition, this unit has reverted to carrying the machine-gun in a scabbard attached to the right side of the 1st gunner's saddle behind the rider. Russia 1941.

Left:
An Hf 1 light field wagon in the train of a horse troop. The men gladly took advantage of long marches to read the army newspaper.
(15th Cavalry Regiment)

Left:
In 1939 both horse regiments and several cavalry regiments were issued the SdKfz 221 for use as an armored scout car. Russia 1942. (6th Cavalry Regiment)

Right:
A horse troop in the winter of 1941 near Moscow. The only winter clothing available to the troopers was the cloth greatcoat and head warmer. (18th Cavalry Regiment)

Left:
Better winter clothing was available by the winter of 1942-43, but improvisation was still required in order to ensure that the 37-mm anti-tank guns of the 3rd (Heavy) Troops retained their mobility. (6th Cavalry Regiment)

Of this the General der Inf. im OKH - I Kav noted in February 1945: "It is especially tragic that this proven division was reorganized as a panzer division shortly before the point in time when the conditions in the autumn of 1941 would have given a cavalry unit an extensive field of activity. One can only understand why the cavalry division, which always operated with armored units, gave up its horses by examine the contemporary contexts of the lightning campaigns and the overestimation of technical means."

Meanwhile the SS-Verfügungstruppe, which later became the Waffen-SS, established two SS-Horse Regiments from a starting point of zero, meaning without active cadres or detachments from other units. The two regiments were used to create an SS Cavalry Brigade. The unit, which distinguished itself in action, especially at Rzhev, was also expanded into a division. When the divisions of the Waffen-SS were numbered, it was assigned the designation 8th SS Cavalry Division Florian Geyer. From it emerged the 22nd SS Volunteer Cavalry Division Maria Theresia in early 1944. Both divisions were largely destroyed in the Budapest pocket at the beginning of 1945. Afterwards the 37th SS Cavalry Division Lützow was activated for a short time.

In 1943 General von Pannwitz succeeded in assembling a Cossack Cavalry Division from various cossack formations. By 1945 it developed into the VXth Cossack Cavalry Corps with two cavalry divisions and one infantry brigade.

THE REBIRTH OF THE CAVALRY 1943-1945

The year 1942 marked the low point of the cavalry in the German Army. A reorganization of the (remnant) reconnaissance battalions in a cavalry sense or the resurrection of army cavalry units was not under debate. On the other hand the 8th SS Cavalry Division Florian Geyer continued to demonstrate that army cavalry could be employed with success under the terrain and climatic conditions of Russia, although to some degree it exhibited the same structural shortcomings that the army's 1st Cavalry Division had done earlier. Then, in late 1942, Rittmeister Georg Freiherr von Boeselager succeeded in convincing the Commander in Chief of Army Group Center, Generalfeldmarschall von Kluge, that a horse-mounted unit suitable for reconnaissance and combat tasks would be an asset to the army group in the existing situation. In spite of the difficulties to be expected in forming such a unit in the fourth year of the war, Generalfeldmarschall von Kluge approved Rittmeister von Boeselager's proposal. And so, quite contrary to expectations, "Cavalry Unit Boeselager" was created by an army group order dated January 14, 1943. The units which made up the formation were initially horse squadrons from the reconnaissance battalions which were withdrawn from the front-line areas of Army Group Center.

Soon, at the end of March 1943, the formation was expanded into a regiment dubbed Cavalry Regiment Center, and in the following months the other two army

Close-up of a cavalry section of the 1st Cavalry Division in Russia in 1941. The photograph provides an extremely clear view of the section's arms and equipment as well as the manner in which they were carried in wartime. It is interesting to note that the trooper on the right of the photo has Type 34 saddlebags on the front of the saddle as well as the new type saddlebags behind.

Above:
A troop of the 1st Cavalry Division moves out to attack at dawn. Visible in the center of the photo is an MG 34 loaded on a pack horse.

Above:
Horse-drawn anti-tank platoon of the 1s Cavalry Division. The gunners ride, while ammunition for the guns is carried by pack horses.

Right:
An If 8 infantry cart in use as a means of transport by the cavalry division.

groups, North and South, also received similar cavalry regiments. Although neither at full strength or suitably equipped, these regiments achieved such success that the Chief of the Army General Staff, Generaloberst Zeitzler, had plans worked out for the formation of an Army Cavalry Corps.

Effective May 3, 1944, therefore, the three cavalry regiments were reorganized into two cavalry brigades. Together with an Hungarian cavalry division they formed the Ist (Army) Cavalry Corps. Elements of the corps played a not inconsiderable role in stabilizing the situation following the collapse of Army Group Center in June 1944.

After a brief period of action in the defense of East Prussia, the Cavalry Corps was transferred to Hungary. There it took part in the last major offensive by the Wehrmacht; code-named "Spring Awakening," it was supposed to regain the Danube Line.

Although the offensive was a complete success at first, after ten days it literally became stuck in the mud.

As per a decree by the OKH on February 23, 1945, both brigades were raised to the level of divisions without receiving any significant reinforcements. The cavalry divisions carried out a fighting withdrawal in the direction of the frontier of the Reich until the end of the war, and following the German surrender they were interned by the English in Austria. The English handed them over to the Americans. In this way they ended up "man, horse and wagon" in the American occupation zone. There the horses were distributed for use in agriculture and soon afterward the soldiers and officers were released to return to their homes. With this the German cavalry had ceased to exist.

The vehicle of the commanding officer of Cavalry Regiment Center. On the left fender is the unit's command pennant. Russia 1943.

Command post of the 3rd Cavalry Brigade in August 1944.

Above right:
Commanding officer of the 3rd Cavalry Brigade, Oberstleutnant von Boeselager, wearing the old style garrison cap. Although procurement officially ended on 1/4/1942, these popular caps were worn until the end of the war.

A cavalry troop of the army cavalry, which was reestablished in 1943. Stick-type hand grenades were often strapped to the Type 34 saddlebags.

43

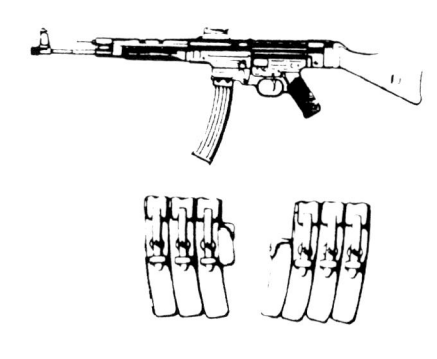

Left and above:
In 1944 the riflemen of the horse troops began receiving the Sturmgewehr 44 assault rifle. (5th Cavalry Regiment)

Left:
In the 41st Horse Regiment the new weapon was carried barrel-down. This method of carriage, disapproved of by the Wehrmacht, proved less disturbing to the rider while on horseback.

Left:
radio station of the 31st Horse Regiment with Type B backpack radio set. In the background is the set's pack horse. Clearly visible is the breeching of the Type 33 pack saddle.

The command armored troop carrier (SdKfz 251) of the commanding officer of the 3rd Cavalry Brigade in August 1944.

The 80-mm mortar was the horse regiment's heaviest weapon. Each mortar troop had twelve mortars, which were transported in horse-drawn vehicles. (32nd Horse Regiment)

The Cavalry Brigade's heaviest unit was the Anti-tank Battalion, which was equipped with thirty-one assault guns and twelve 20-mm flak on self-propelled carriages. Here a StuG III Ausf D with the short-barrelled 75-mm gun (24 calibers), which was called the "Stummel" (stump).

45

The 8th SS Cavalry Division Florian Geyer at the Dniepr River in 1943. Troops of this regiment wore the garrison cap for NCOs and men with the camouflage tunic.

Below: More typical for the cavalry of the Waffen-SS, however, was the standard garrison cap (with peak) in camouflage colors.

Mounted 1-3 radio team of the 1st SS Horse Regiment with Type b1 backpack radio loaded on a pack horse. The leader of the radio team is missing from the photo.

Above right: Unterscharführer (sergeant) of the 1st SS Horse Regiment. When formed in 1939-40, the equipment and weapons of the cavalry of the later Waffen-SS differed little from that of the army.

Right: In 1942 troopers of the Waffen-SS began wearing camouflage tunics and camouflage covers for the Stahlhelm 35 helmet.

Members of the 1st Cossack Cavalry Division, established in 1943, are sworn in. The cossacks wore German uniforms with traditional fur caps and emblems. Armament was non-uniform and riding tack was more or less left to the troopers themselves.

Cossack troop engaged in anti-partisan duties in Croatia in 1944. The troop commander is armed with a Russian submachine-gun and the men with the Karabiner 98k.